Ultimate Travel Guide To

CAIRNS, Australia

*Don't Book Your Cairns Trip
Without This Guide:
Everything You Need Awaits!*

Elizabeth Whyte

Copyright Notice

This publication is copyright protected. This is only for personal use. No part of this publication may be, including but not limited to, reproduced, in any form or medium, stored in a data retrieval system or transmitted by or through any means, without prior written permission from the Author / Publisher.

Legal action will be pursued if this is breached.

SCAN TO SEE ALL MY BOOKS

DISCLAIMER

Please note that the information contained within this document is for educational purposes only. The information contained herein has been obtained from sources believed to be reliable at the time of publication. The opinions expressed herein are subject to change without notice.

Readers acknowledge that the Author / Publisher is not engaging in rendering legal, financial or professional advice. The Publisher / Author disclaims all warranties as to the accuracy, completeness, or adequacy of such information.

The Publisher assumes no liability for errors, omissions, or inadequacies in the information contained herein or from the interpretations thereof. The publisher / Author specifically disclaims any liability from the use or application of the information contained herein or from the interpretations thereof.

TABLE OF CONTENT

Copyright Notice
Disclaimer
Table of Content
Introduction
Welcome to the Ultimate Travel Guide to Cairns, Australia

   Why Cairns?

   Discovering the Tropical Paradise

   How to Use This Guide: Your Roadmap to an Unforgettable Cairns Adventure

Chapter 1
Getting Acquainted with Cairns

   Cairns: Where the Reef Meets the Rainforest

   A Brief History of Cairns

   Climate and Best Travel Period

   Geography and Layout of Cairns

Chapter 2
Preparing for Your Cairns Adventure

   Travel Essentials: Visas, Currency, and Language

   Vaccinations and Health Precautions

   Packing Tips for Your Cairns Trip

   Budgeting for Your Cairns Adventure

Chapter 3

Navigating Cairns

Transportation Options:

How to Get to Cairns

Public Transportation and Rental Cars for Getting Around Cairns

Maps and Apps You Need

to Explore Cairns

Options for Lodging:

Hotels, Resorts, and Hostels

Chapter 4
Must-See Attractions in Cairns

Cairns Esplanade: The Heart of the City

The Great Barrier Reef: A Natural Wonder

Kuranda: A Journey into the Rainforest

Daintree Rainforest:

An Ancient Wonderland

Tjapukai Aboriginal Cultural Park: Discover Indigenous Culture

Cairns Aquarium:

Exploring Marine Life

Chapter 5
Outdoor Adventures in Cairns

Snorkeling and Scuba Diving

on the Great Barrier Reef

Rainforest Hiking and Wildlife Encounters

White Water Rafting on the Tully River

Table of Contents

    Skydiving and Bungee Jumping in Cairns

    Exploring the Atherton Tablelands

    Horseback Riding and ATV Tours

Chapter 6
Food, Dining, and Nightlife

    A Culinary Journey in Cairns:

    Must-Try Dishes

    Best Restaurants and Cafes in Cairns

    Nightlife in Cairns:

    Bars, Clubs, and Entertainment

    Local Markets and Gastronomic Adventures

Chapter 7
Cultural Immersion

    Learning About Indigenous Cultures

    Events and Festivals in Cairns

    Arts and Museums in the City

    Volunteering and Sustainable Tourism

Chapter 8
Day Trips and Nearby Destinations

    Port Douglas: Relaxation and Luxury

    Palm Cove: A Beachside Escape

    Fitzroy Island: Paradise Just Off the Coast

    Cape Tribulation:

    Where Rainforest Meets Reef

    Exploring the Outback:

Undara Lava Tubes

The Undiscovered Gem: Babinda Boulders

Chapter 9
Practical Tips and Safety

Staying Safe in Cairns:

Health and Safety Guidelines

Money Matters:

Currency Exchange and ATMs

Communication and Internet Access

Local Laws and Etiquette

Environmental Responsibility:

Protecting the Reef and Rainforest

Chapter 10
Itineraries for Every Traveler

One-Week Adventure:

A Quick Taste of Cairns

Two-Week Explorer:

Delving Deeper into Cairns and Beyond

Family-Friendly Cairns:

Activities for Kids

Romantic Getaway:

Cairns for Couples

Solo Traveler's Cairns:

Embrace the Adventure

Chapter 11
Resources and Additional Information

Useful Websites and Apps

for Cairns Travel

Booking Tours and Activities

Traveler's Checklist: What Not to Forget

Reader's Stories:

Personal Cairns Adventures

Contact Information for

Local Authorities and Embassies

Conclusion
Farewell to Cairns: A Memorable Experience

Sharing Your Cairns Adventure

Keep Exploring:

Your Travel Journey Continues

Introduction

WELCOME TO THE ULTIMATE TRAVEL GUIDE TO CAIRNS, AUSTRALIA

Are you ready to embark on an unforgettable vacation to a tropical paradise? Look no further than Cairns, a breathtaking destination nestled in the very heart of Australia's Queensland region.

Whether you're an adventure seeker, nature lover, or someone in search of a perfect beachside getaway, Cairns has something UNIQUE to offer.

Why Cairns?
Discovering the Tropical Paradise

So, why should you choose Cairns for your next vacation or adventure? Well, let me paint a picture for you.

I want you to imagine a place where lush rainforests collide with the world's most famous coral reef, where you can explore vibrant underwater ecosystems in the morning and hike through ancient jungles in the afternoon.

Cairns is where the Great Barrier Reef meets the Daintree Rainforest, creating a unique fusion of natural wonders that will leave you awe-inspired.

But Cairns is not just about its stunning landscapes. It's also a place where you can immerse yourself in indigenous cultures, savor mouthwatering cuisine, and experience a vibrant nightlife scene.

Whether you're traveling alone, with family, or on a romantic getaway, Cairns has activities and attractions that cater to all manner of travelers.

How to Use This Guide: Your Roadmap to an Unforgettable Cairns Adventure

Now, you might be wondering how to make the most of your Cairns adventure. This Ultimate Travel Guide can help with that.. We've meticulously crafted this guide to be your go-to resource for everything Cairns-related.

Each chapter of this guide is packed with valuable information to help you plan your trip. Here's a sneak preview of what to expect:

Chapter 1: Getting Acquainted with Cairns - Learn about the history, climate, and layout of Cairns, so you can get a sense of this enchanting city.

Chapter 2: Preparing for Your Cairns Adventure - Get practical advice on visas, health precautions, packing tips, and budgeting for your trip.

Chapter 3: Navigating Cairns - Discover the best transportation options, how to get around the city, and where to stay.

Chapter 4: Must-See Attractions in Cairns - Dive into the top attractions, from the iconic Great Barrier Reef to the cultural experiences awaiting you.

Chapter 5: Outdoor Adventures in Cairns - Find your inner adventurer with snorkeling, hiking, rafting, skydiving, and more.

Chapter 6: Food, Dining, and Nightlife - Delight your taste buds with Cairns' culinary scene and explore its vibrant nightlife.

Chapter 7: Cultural Immersion - Learn about the rich Indigenous cultures, festivals, arts, and volunteering opportunities in Cairns.

Chapter 8: Day Trips and Nearby Destinations - Plan unforgettable day trips to nearby gems like Port Douglas, Palm Cove, and Cape Tribulation.

Chapter 9: Practical Tips and Safety - Stay safe, manage your finances, and understand local customs and environmental responsibility.

Chapter 10: Itineraries for Every Traveler - Whether you have a week or just a weekend, we've got itineraries for all types of travelers.

Chapter 11: Resources and Additional Information - Access useful websites, booking tips, checklists, and even read personal stories from fellow travelers.

In the end, we hope this guide helps you craft an unforgettable Cairns adventure that suits your style and preferences. So, get ready to explore this tropical paradise, create lasting memories, and share your Cairns adventure with us!

Now, let's dive into the heart of Cairns and make your travel dreams come true. Your adventure begins here!

Chapter 1

GETTING ACQUAINTED WITH CAIRNS

Welcome to Chapter 1 of the Ultimate Travel Guide to Cairns!! I'll be introducing you to the awesome city of Cairns, which is situated where the Reef and the Rainforest converge.

Together, we'll delve into the geology, history, and climate of this tropical haven to provide you with a solid foundation for your Cairns journey.

Cairns: Where the Reef Meets the Rainforest

There is nowhere else in the world like Cairns. The Great Barrier Reef and the Daintree Rainforest meet here, making it one of Mother Nature's most magnificent creations.

Cairns is a truly tropical wonderland thanks to this extraordinary mix of marine and terrestrial ecosystems.

Imagine starting your day diving in the Great Barrier Reef's beautiful coral gardens and ending it by hiking through ancient rainforests that have been standing for millions of years. Cairns is a haven for lovers of the outdoors and thrill-seekers alike since it offers the best of both worlds.

A Brief History of Cairns

It's important to understand a little bit of Cairns' history before you immerse yourself in its natural splendor. Originally home to the native Yirrganydji people, Cairns became a bustling port city in the late 19th century as a result of the finding of gold in the surrounding region.

William Wellington Cairns, who was the governor of Queensland at the time, inspired the city's name.

Over time, Cairns has transformed into a thriving, multiethnic city that honors its indigenous roots and acts as a starting point for exploring the beauties of the surrounding area.

Today, it serves as a destination for adventurers as well as a community that values its rich cultural diversity and historical past.

Climate and Best Travel Period

Due to its tropical climate, Cairns has warm temperatures all year long. However, it's imperative to schedule your trip around the seasons.

The dry season, which normally lasts from April to November, is the busiest travel period. The weather during this time is perfect for outdoor sports like diving and snorkeling.

The wet season, which lasts from December to March, can be a good time to visit if you want a more sedate and affordable experience. The verdant landscapes are at their most brilliant during this time, despite the occasional rain showers that are common, and you can still enjoy many activities with less people.

Geography and Layout of Cairns

You can get around Cairns more efficiently if you know its layout and geography. Cairns is located on Queensland's east coast, facing the Coral Sea. The bustling Cairns Esplanade and the waterfront are easily accessible from the city core, which is tucked away along the coast.

As you wander the city, you'll come across a blend of cutting-edge construction and breathtaking scenery.

The Great Dividing Range's beautiful mountains are to the west, while the Great Barrier Reef, which is famous across the world, is to the north.

Due to its convenient location close to the city core, tourists from all over the world may easily access the Cairns International Airport.

Having had a taste of Cairns, you're ready to start seriously preparing for your vacation.

We'll go over everything from the most important aspects of travel to the must-see sights and outdoor activities that this tropical paradise has to offer in the future chapters.

Prepare yourself to discover Cairns in a new way!

Chapter 2

PREPARING FOR YOUR CAIRNS ADVENTURE

Welcome to Chapter 2, where I'll make sure you're fully prepared for your Cairns adventure.

From essential travel documents to health precautions, packing tips, and budgeting advice, I've got you covered.

Travel Essentials: Visas, Currency, and Language

Let's start with the basics. Before jetting off to Cairns, make sure you have the following travel essentials in order:

Visas: You may be needing a visa to enter Australia depending on your nationality. Check the Australian government's official website or consult your nearest Australian embassy or consulate to find out the specific visa requirements for your country.

Ensure you apply for your visa well in advance to avoid any last-minute hassles.

Currency: Australia's official currency is the Australian Dollar (AUD). While credit cards are widely accepted in Cairns, it's a good idea to carry some cash for small purchases and emergencies.

You can exchange currency at banks, exchange bureaus, and even ATMs.

Language: English is the official language in Australia. You'll have no trouble communicating with locals, but it's always fun to learn a few Aussie slang words like "G'day" (hello) and "mate" (friend).

Vaccinations and Health Precautions

Your health and well-being during your Cairns adventure are of utmost importance. Here are some health considerations:

Vaccinations: Depending on your previous travel history and health conditions, you might need vaccinations or preventive measures.

Consult your doctor or a travel health clinic well before your trip to discuss vaccinations for diseases such as Hepatitis A, Hepatitis B, and Typhoid.

Travel Insurance: Consider purchasing comprehensive travel insurance that covers medical emergencies, trip cancellations, and lost luggage.

It's a safety net that can provide peace of mind during your travels.

Sun Protection: Cairns has a sunny tropical climate, so be sure to pack sunscreen, sunglasses, and a wide-brimmed hat to protect yourself from the sun's strong rays.

Water Safety: If you plan to swim or snorkel, be aware of the potential for stingers (jellyfish) during certain times of the year.

Check local advisories and swim at designated safe areas.

Packing Tips for Your Cairns Trip

Packing for Cairns requires a mix of tropical essentials and outdoor adventure gear. Here is a checklist to assist you in packing wisely:

Light Clothing: Cairns is warm year-round, so pack lightweight, breathable clothing. Don't forget your swimwear, as you'll likely be spending a lot of time in the water.

Hiking Gear: If you plan to explore the rainforests or take on any hiking trails, bring comfortable hiking shoes, insect repellent, and a daypack for essentials like water and snacks.

Snorkeling/Diving Gear: If you're an avid snorkeler or diver, consider bringing your own equipment, including a mask, snorkel, and reef-safe sunscreen. However, rental gear is readily available if you prefer to travel light.

Electronics: Don't forget your camera or smartphone for capturing the incredible landscapes. An adapter for Australian electrical outlets is also handy.

Travel Adapter: Since Australia uses different plug types (Type I), make sure you have the right adapter for your electronic devices.

Reusable Water Bottle: Cairns is hot, and you'll want to stay hydrated. Carry a reusable water bottle to fill up throughout the day.

Travel Documents: Keep your passport, visa, travel insurance details, and any other important documents in a secure, waterproof pouch.

Budgeting for Your Cairns Adventure

Cairns can be as budget-friendly or as luxurious as you desire. Here are some budgeting tips to help you make the most of your adventure:

Accommodation: Cairns offers a range of accommodation options, from budget hostels to luxury resorts. To get the best prices, do your research and make your reservations early.

Dining: Enjoying local cuisine at restaurants and cafes is part of the Cairns experience. Budget-conscious travelers can also find affordable eats at food markets and street vendors.

Activities: Plan your activities in advance and look for combo deals that bundle multiple experiences. Remember, many natural attractions like the beaches and rainforests are free to explore.

Transport: Consider using public transport or renting a car, depending on your itinerary. Public buses and ferries are convenient and cost-effective for getting around Cairns.

Tipping: Tipping is not compulsory in Australia, but it's appreciated for good service. It's generally not expected at cafes or casual dining places.

With your travel essentials sorted, health precautions taken, and packing list ready, you're well on your way to an unforgettable Cairns adventure.

In the upcoming chapters, I'll guide you through transportation options, must-see attractions, outdoor adventures, and more.

So, get ready to explore this tropical paradise without a worry in the world!

Chapter 3

NAVIGATING CAIRNS

Welcome to Chapter 3, where I'll show you how to easily get around Cairns. I have all the information you need, including directions, how to get around, and where to stay.

Transportation Options: How to Get to Cairns

The first exciting stage of your adventure is getting to Cairns. Consider the following options for transportation:

By Air: Cairns International Airport (CNS) serves as the primary point of entry for most visitors from abroad. Direct flights are offered by numerous airlines from significant cities all around the world.

Domestic flights from Australian cities like Sydney, Melbourne, and Brisbane to Cairns are another option if you're coming from there.

By Sea: Cairns has a busy port if you're coming from one of the neighbouring islands or even from Papua New Guinea. Here, cruise ships frequently dock, providing a distinctive opportunity to explore the city.

By Road: You can get to Cairns by automobile if you're driving down the coast or touring other regions of Queensland.

The major road into Cairns is the Bruce Highway, and the trip provides beautiful coastal vistas.

By Bus: Cairns is connected to other significant Queensland cities by long-distance bus services. If you're not in a hurry and want to take in the landscape, it's an economical mode of transportation.

Public Transportation and Rental Cars for Getting Around Cairns

Once you've reached Cairns, you'll need a dependable means of transportation to go around the city and explore its environs. The following are your options:

Public Transportation: Cairns has a reliable bus system as well as a light rail system known as the "Cairns Sunbus." Numerous important city attractions are conveniently accessible with the Sunbus. The Sunbus can be used to get to the local suburbs and beaches.

Rental Cars: Renting a car is a practical choice if you intend to thoroughly explore Cairns and the surrounding area. Rental companies can be found all across the city, including the Cairns Airport. It's important to remember that Australians drive on the left side of the road.

Taxis and rideshares: Cairns has an abundance of taxis and rideshare companies like Uber. They are practical for quick travels inside the city.

Bicycles: Cairns has designated bike lanes and rental facilities, making it a bike-friendly city. A fun and environmentally friendly way to tour the city and its beautiful bike trails is by renting a bike.

Walking: The Cairns city center is a great place to explore on foot because it is fairly small. Walking makes it simple to explore local markets, meander along the Cairns Esplanade, and find undiscovered gems.

Maps and Apps You Need to Explore Cairns

Take into account these necessary maps and software to make getting around Cairns even simpler:

To assist you navigate the city's streets, get a copy of the Cairns street map or download one from the internet. It helps you navigate Cairns's downtown area.

Google Maps: For real-time information on public transportation alternatives, routes, and surrounding attractions, turn to the dependable Google Maps app.

Cairns Transport Apps: Public transportation in Cairns is accessible via a number of apps, including the Sunbus app, which offers real-time bus monitoring and timetable information.

Tourist Information Centers: There are various tourist information centers in Cairns where you can pick up free maps and brochures. These facilities are a great resource for organizing your activities.

Options for Lodging: Hotels, Resorts, and Hostels

Your experience in Cairns can be substantially improved by picking the proper lodging. Here is a list of choices:

Hotels and Resorts: Cairns provides a variety of hotels and resorts to accommodate different tastes and budgets. There are many options available, whether you choose to stay in an opulent beachfront hotel or a quaint boutique hotel in the heart of the city.

Hostels: There are numerous hostels in Cairns for tourists on a tight budget. Hostels are an excellent choice for backpackers and lone travelers because they are not only inexpensive but also provide a social environment.

Holiday Apartments: If you want to feel like you're at home away from home, think about renting a holiday apartment. These include living areas, fully functional kitchens, and occasionally even individual balconies.

Resorts and Spa Retreats: Cairns is renowned for its opulent resorts and spa getaways. These are excellent for traveling in style or for couples searching for a romantic break.

Camping & Caravan Parks: Cairns offers a number of picturesque camping and caravan parks for outdoor enthusiasts. Some are located close to lakes, forests, or beaches.

Any sort of lodging you want should be reserved in advance, especially during the busiest travel times. When choosing, take into account your preferences for location, your spending limit, and the things that are most important to you.

You're ready to start exploring this tropical paradise with confidence now that you're well-prepared with transit alternatives, understand how to navigate around Cairns, have access to key maps and applications, and are aware of your lodging possibilities.

We'll delve into the must-see sights, outdoor activities, and gastronomic treats that Cairns has to offer in the following chapters.

So, get ready for an amazing journey!

Chapter 4

MUST-SEE ATTRACTIONS IN CAIRNS

Welcome to Chapter 4, where I'll give you a tour of some of Cairns's most fascinating and important sights.

Every traveler may find something to enjoy in Cairns, from the city's center to its natural attractions and cultural experiences.

Cairns Esplanade: The Heart of the City

Let's start with the vibrant heart of Cairns, the Cairns Esplanade. This bustling waterfront area offers a little something for everyone:

Lagoon Swimming: Cool off in the crystal-clear waters of the Cairns Esplanade Lagoon. Since it is surrounded by lush parkland and sandy shores, it is a favored place for both locals and tourists.

Walking and Biking: Take a leisurely stroll or rent a bike to explore the scenic esplanade. During your trip, you'll pass by lovely gardens, fitness facilities, and lots of spots to unwind.

Cafes and Restaurants: Satisfy your taste buds at the numerous cafes and restaurants overlooking the Coral Sea. This is where you can savor fresh seafood and other culinary delights.

Art Markets: On weekends, the Esplanade comes alive with local artisans selling their crafts and creations at the Cairns Esplanade Markets. You can find some nice souvenirs there.

Live Entertainment: Keep an eye out for live music and cultural performances that often take place at the esplanade. It's an excellent way to become fully immersed in the community's culture.

The Great Barrier Reef: A Natural Wonder

Now, for the jewel in Cairns' crown - the Great Barrier Reef. This UNESCO World Heritage-listed marvel is the world's largest coral reef system and an absolute must-see:

Snorkeling and Diving: Dive or snorkel amidst the colorful corals and an array of marine life. The reef is teeming with fish, turtles, and even the occasional reef shark.

Boat Tours: Many tour operators offer boat trips to the reef, providing opportunities for snorkeling, diving, and even semi-submersible rides for those who prefer to stay dry.

Helicopter Tours: Get a bird's-eye view of the reef by taking a scenic helicopter ride. It's an amazing way to appreciate the vastness and magnificence of this natural marvel.

Island Retreats: Visit nearby islands like Green Island or Fitzroy Island, which offer a more relaxed way to experience the reef. You can snorkel, hike, or simply bask in the sun.

Kuranda: A Journey into the Rainforest

Escape to the lush rainforest village of Kuranda, nestled in the mountains just a short drive or scenic train ride from Cairns:

Scenic Railway: Hop aboard the Kuranda Scenic Railway for a journey through dense rainforests, steep ravines, and thundering waterfalls. The views are mesmerizing.

Skyrail Rainforest Cableway: Alternatively, take the Skyrail Cableway, which glides above the treetops, offering spectacular panoramas of the rainforest.

Kuranda Village: Explore the quaint village of Kuranda, known for its vibrant markets, wildlife parks, and cultural experiences.

Daintree Rainforest: An Ancient Wonderland

For a truly ancient and untouched experience, head north to the Daintree Rainforest:

Mossman Gorge: Discover the serene Mossman Gorge, a sacred site for the indigenous Kuku Yalanji people. Take a guided walk to learn about the unique ecosystem.

Daintree River Cruise: Spot crocodiles and other wildlife on a Daintree River cruise. It's a wonderful way to take in the thick mangroves and abundant flora.

Cape Tribulation: Reach the iconic Cape Tribulation, where the rainforest meets the reef. Explore pristine beaches and hiking trails in this stunning wilderness area.

Tjapukai Aboriginal Cultural Park: Discover Indigenous Culture

To immerse yourself in the rich indigenous culture of the region, a visit to the Tjapukai Aboriginal Cultural Park is a must:

Cultural Performances: Experience captivating performances that showcase traditional dances, music, and storytelling.

Art and Craft Demonstrations: Witness the creation of traditional art and crafts, and even try your hand at painting or boomerang throwing.

Bush Tucker Dining: Savor native Australian flavors with a bush tucker-inspired meal. It's a culinary journey that highlights indigenous ingredients.

Cairns Aquarium: Exploring Marine Life

The Cairns Aquarium is a great place to go if you want to learn more about marine life without getting wet:

Aquatic Exhibits: Explore a variety of painstakingly replicated aquatic ecosystems, such as the Great

Barrier Reef, the Daintree Rainforest, and more, at the aquatic exhibits.

Interactive Displays: Get up close to a variety of marine creatures, from colorful corals and reef fish to freshwater turtles and sharks.

Educational Presentations and Programs: The aquarium offers enlightening talks and educational activities, making it a fantastic destination for families and anybody with a passion for marine biology.

These must-see sights are only the beginning of Cairns' attractions. The enthralling outdoor activities, mouthwatering dining opportunities, and cultural immersion that are waiting for you in this tropical paradise will all be covered in the future chapters.

So, get ready to explore Cairns even more!

Chapter 5

OUTDOOR ADVENTURES IN CAIRNS

The heart-pounding, nature-exploring, and adrenaline-pumping outdoor activities that Cairns has to offer will be covered in detail in this chapter. Prepare for a once-in-a-lifetime adventure!

Snorkeling and Scuba Diving on the Great Barrier Reef

Let's begin with the Great Barrier Reef tour, which is the most well-known excursion in Cairns:

Snorkeling: Without much training, snorkeling is the best option for individuals who wish to get up close and personal with the colorful marine life of the reef. Just put on your mask, snorkel, and fins to enter an aquatic world.

Scuba diving: Cairns has some of the top dive locations in the world if you're a certified diver or eager to become one. Explore the depths to find intricate coral formations and the varied marine ecology, which includes elusive reef sharks, beautiful turtles, and colorful fish.

Liveaboard Tours: If you want to spend more time exploring various dive sites on the reef, think about signing up for a liveaboard cruise. These extended journeys provide an immersive experience.

Rainforest Hiking and Wildlife Encounters

In addition to the water, Cairns is bordered by magnificent rainforests bursting with life.

Hiking Trails: Explore the countless hiking routes in the Wet Tropics World Heritage Area. Fantastic choices include Mossman Gorge and the Daintree Rainforest. Don't forget to look out for unique plants and animals along the trip.

Wildlife Watching: A wonderful variety of wildlife may be found in Cairns. Join a guided trip to see local animals like cassowaries, tree kangaroos, and vibrant wildlife. To see the rainforest come to life at night, go on a nocturnal wildlife trip.

Ziplining and Canopy Walks: Get an adrenaline thrill while seeing the rainforest canopy from above with ziplining and canopy walks. There are attractions like ziplining and canopy walks that offer a distinctive view of the rainforest.

White Water Rafting on the Tully River

Are you prepared for some exciting action? You'll never forget the thrill of white-water rafting on the Tully River:

Rapids Galore: The Tully River is renowned for its exhilarating rapids, making it a top destination for white water rafting enthusiasts. There is a journey for everyone, regardless of skill level.

Stunning Scenery: Take a moment to take in the breathtaking rainforest scenery as you make your way through the rapids.

Safety First: You can relax knowing that knowledgeable guides will be with you at all times, ensuring your security while maximizing your fun.

Skydiving and Bungee Jumping in Cairns

Cairns offers some thrilling options if you're a daredevil or want to overcome your fear of heights:

Skydiving: Jump out of a plane over the city to get the biggest rush ever. The aerial views of Cairns, the reef, and the rainforest are absolutely unforgettable.

Bungee jumping: Visit the nearby AJ Hackett Cairns to jump off a specially constructed tower. You'll be giddy with excitement as you experience the rush of freefall and rebounding.

Exploring the Atherton Tablelands

Discover the Atherton Tablelands, a picturesque highland area full of natural attractions, by traveling inland:

Waterfalls: The Atherton Tablelands are home to numerous magnificent waterfalls, including Millaa Millaa Falls and Josephine Falls. Swimming and picnicking are both great activities at these cascades.

Volcanic Craters: Explore historic volcanic craters like Lake Eacham and Lake Barrine. These tranquil crater lakes are perfect for swimming, and there are walking trails that allow you to explore the nearby jungle.

Wildlife and Dairy Farms: Visit dairy farms to experience delectable regional cheeses. Keep a watch out for animals; you might see tree kangaroos, platypuses, and vibrant parrots.

Horseback Riding and ATV Tours

Get in the saddle or climb aboard an ATV for a new kind of adventure:

Horseback Riding: Riding a horse lets you take in the splendor of a rainforest or the excitement of a beach ride. It's a special way to engage with nature.

ATV Tours: If you'd like a little bit more speed, you can go on an ATV tour through off-road and rainforest terrain. Get ready to have fun and get dirty.

You're in for an exciting voyage with these outdoor activities in Cairns.

Cairns offers an outdoor experience for any thrill-seeker and nature lover, whether you're scuba diving into the Great Barrier Reef's depths, hiking through ancient rainforests, overcoming rapids, taking a leap of faith, discovering interior delights, or enjoying a special ride.

The chapters that follow will tempt your taste buds with gastronomic treats and introduce you to the rich cultural experiences this tropical paradise has in store for you.

Prepare yourself for more Cairns adventure!

Chapter 6

FOOD, DINING, AND NIGHTLIFE

Welcome to Chapter 6, where we'll embark on a delicious tour of Cairns' culinary delights.

Cairns has a lot to offer in terms of dining, entertainment, and must-try foods, in addition to the top restaurants and a buzzing nightlife.

A Culinary Journey in Cairns: Must-Try Dishes

Let's start with the flavors of Cairns. The city's diverse culinary scene reflects its multicultural makeup, and there are some dishes you simply can't wait to try out:

Barramundi: Cairns is known for its succulent barramundi fish, often grilled or pan-fried to perfection. It's a must-try for seafood lovers.

Kangaroo: For a true taste of Australia, sample kangaroo meat, typically served as a steak or in a gourmet dish.

Prawn and Mango Salad: Enjoy the tropical flavors of Cairns with a refreshing prawn and mango salad, often paired with a zesty dressing.

Crocodile: If you're feeling adventurous, try crocodile meat. It's lean and has a mild, chicken-like flavor. It's often served as a kebab or in a burger.

Tropical Fruits: Cairns is surrounded by tropical fruit farms, so be sure to indulge in fresh fruits like mangoes, papayas, and lychees.

Barron River Mud Crab: Feast on the flavorful mud crab, a Cairns specialty. It's best enjoyed steamed or in a chili crab dish.

Australian Beef: Australia is renowned for its beef, so savor a juicy steak from a local grill or steakhouse.

Damper: For a taste of traditional Australian bush food, try damper, a type of bush bread often served with golden syrup.

Best Restaurants and Cafes in Cairns

Cairns boasts a vibrant dining scene with a variety of culinary experiences to suit all tastes and budgets:

Salt House: Enjoy waterfront dining at Salt House, known for its seafood, cocktails, and stunning views of the marina.

Ochre Restaurant: Ochre Restaurant is a premier destination for native-inspired cuisine that creatively uses local Australian products.

Waterbar & Grill Steakhouse: For some of the best steaks in town, visit Waterbar & Grill Steakhouse if you're a fan of the meat.

Caffiend: Coffee lovers will appreciate Caffiend for its specialty brews and cozy ambiance.

Bang & Grind: This hip cafe serves scrumptious sandwiches, brunch dishes, and a variety of vegetarian and vegan options.

Night Markets: Cairns Night Markets are a foodie's paradise with stalls offering everything from Thai and Japanese to Indian and Italian cuisine.

Local Eateries: Don't miss the opportunity to try local eats at casual dining spots and food stalls. Look out for fish and chips shops, kebab stands, and bakeries serving fresh meat pies.

Nightlife in Cairns: Bars, Clubs, and Entertainment

Cairns doesn't sleep after the sun sets. Here's a taste of the nightlife scene:

The Pier Bar: Sip cocktails by the waterfront at The Pier Bar, often featuring live music and a lively atmosphere.

Gilligan's Backpacker Hotel & Resort: This vibrant venue offers everything from a relaxed beer garden to a nightclub for those looking to dance the night away.

The Cotton Club: The Cotton Club is a popular hangout because of its welcoming ambiance and wide selection of drinks.

Mad Cow Tavern: For a night of live music, head to Mad Cow Tavern, which hosts bands and DJs throughout the week.

Cairns Dinner Theatre: The Cairns Dinner Theatre offers live performances and themed banquets for a night of exquisite cuisine and entertainment.

Local Markets and Gastronomic Adventures

Investigate Cairns' regional markets and gourmet experiences to fully embrace its culinary culture:

Rusty's Markets: Rusty's Markets is a bustling center open on the weekends where you can experience local handcrafted goods, exotic cuisines, and fresh local produce.

Tjapukai By Night: Tjapukai By Night is a distinctive evening experience where you may sample native cuisine and take in traditional activities.

Cooktown: Take a road trip to Cooktown, where you can eat regional delicacies and see the picturesque countryside.

Cairns Food and Wine Festival: Don't miss the Cairns Food and Wine Festival if it happens to be taking place while you're there. It honors the region's wine and culinary traditions.

With its natural beauty, Cairns is not only a feast for the eyes, but also a feast for the palate. Every food enthusiast will find something to enjoy in this city, from regional specialties to international cuisine.

To fully understand the depth of this tropical paradise, we'll explore the rich cultural immersion Cairns has to offer in the future chapters.

Prepare for additional exploration!

Chapter 7

CULTURAL IMMERSION

We'll delve deeply into the numerous options for rich cultural immersion that Cairns offers in this chapter. There is so much to learn about, from vibrant festivals to indigenous cultures, to exploring the city's museums and arts.

Learning About Indigenous Cultures

Considering that Cairns is located on the traditional lands of the Aboriginal and Torres Strait Islander peoples, it's a great site to learn about indigenous cultures:

Tjapukai Aboriginal Cultural Park: We already mentioned this, but it needs repeating. Tjapukai is a unique opportunity to gain knowledge about the oldest continuously existing culture in the world through engaging activities, dance performances, and old-fashioned storytelling.

Indigenous Tours: Take part in guided excursions that take you far into the rainfo and are led by native guides who share their understanding of the geography, its history, and their customs.

Art Centers: Go to art centers where you may view and buy real indigenous artwork, including paintings and handicrafts, including the Mossman Gorge Centre and Djiru National Park.

Events and Festivals in Cairns

Numerous festivals and events are held annually in Cairns, offering a fascinating glimpse into the local way of life and sense of camaraderie:

Cairns Festival: The Cairns Festival is a yearly celebration of the city's artistic, musical, and cultural heritage. A large procession, live concerts, and a bustling multicultural food market are all included.

Cairns Indigenous Art Fair (CIAF): The Cairns Indigenous Art Fair (CIAF) is a significant occasion that highlights the abilities of indigenous musicians, dancers, and artists. It's a chance to interact with the cultures of Aboriginal and Torres Strait Islanders.

Chinese New Year Festival: Due to Cairns' significant Chinese ancestry, this event is a fun celebration that includes dragon dances, traditional Chinese entertainment, and delectable Chinese food.

Palm Cove Reef Feast: The Palm Cove Reef Feast is a gourmet event with a touch of the tropics that takes place in the neighboring Palm Cove. Taste fine cuisine while taking in the coastal ambiance and live music.

Arts and Museums in the City

Cairns has a flourishing artistic community and a number of museums that provide insights into its past and present:

Cairns Art Gallery: Explore modern and native art at the Cairns Art Gallery, which presents exhibitions and events all year round.

KickArts Contemporary Arts: KickArts is devoted to promoting modern visual arts, such as digital art, sculpture, and paintings.

Cairns Museum: The Cairns Museum, housed in a gorgeously restored heritage structure, offers information on the history of Cairns and its early settlers.

Volunteering and Sustainable Tourism

Cairns provides a number of possibilities for visitors interested in supporting sustainability initiatives or giving back to the community:

Volunteer with Conservation Groups: Consider volunteering with local environmental organizations or at a wildlife rehabilitation facility. You may help to preserve the distinctive ecosystems of Cairns by volunteering.

Programs for Reef Conservation: The Great Barrier Reef is the focus of numerous organizations in Cairns. You can help with coral restoration programs or reef cleanliness campaigns.

Sustainable Tours: When visiting the reef and rainforest, pick eco-friendly and sustainable tour providers. Choose tour companies that have emphasis on ethical tourism and environmental conservation.

Indigenous Tourism: Support indigenous-owned companies and tour guides since they often play a key role in safeguarding their cultural heritage and the environment.

Cultural immersion in Cairns is more than just a tourist attraction; it's a chance to get to know the locals, discover historical civilizations, and help to protect this breathtaking tropical paradise.

In the following chapters, we'll go on day tours to surrounding locations and also get helpful tips for a responsible trip to Cairns.

So, get ready to explore this amazing location even more!

Chapter 8

DAY TRIPS AND NEARBY DESTINATIONS

Cairns is not just an awesome location on its own, but the ideal starting point for seeing and touring other nearby locations.

We'll walk you through a few outstanding day adventures from Cairns in this chapter.

Port Douglas: Relaxation and Luxury

Just an hour's drive north of Cairns, you'll find Port Douglas, a picturesque coastal town known for its laid-back vibe and luxury resorts.

Here's what to do in Port Douglas:

Four Mile Beach: Spend your day relaxing on the pristine Four Mile Beach, where you can soak up the sun or take a leisurely walk along the sandy shores.

Great Barrier Reef Tours: Port Douglas offers easy access to the Great Barrier Reef, so consider booking a snorkeling or diving tour from here.

Rainforest Retreats: Explore the nearby Daintree Rainforest or take a guided tour to Mossman Gorge. There are also opportunities for wildlife cruises along the Daintree River.

Macrossan Street: Stroll along Macrossan Street, where you'll find boutique shops, art galleries, and a range of restaurants and cafes.

Palm Cove: A Beachside Escape

Palm Cove, just 25 minutes north of Cairns, is a charming beachside village that exudes tropical tranquility.

Here's what you can enjoy in Palm Cove:

Palm Cove Beach: Relax on the palm-fringed beach or take a dip in the calm waters of the Coral Sea.

Spa Retreats: Pamper yourself at one of the luxury day spas in Palm Cove for a rejuvenating experience.

Esplanade Dining: Enjoy beachfront dining at the esplanade's restaurants and cafes. Fresh seafood is a must-try here.

Tjapukai Aboriginal Cultural Park: On your way to Palm Cove, you can visit the Tjapukai Aboriginal Cultural Park for an enriching cultural experience.

Fitzroy Island: Paradise Just Off the Coast

If you're looking for a tropical paradise within easy reach of Cairns, Fitzroy Island is a gem. It's only a 45-minute ferry ride away and offers:

Snorkeling and Hiking: Explore the underwater wonders by snorkeling off Nudey Beach, or take a hike through the island's lush rainforest.

Glass-Bottom Boat Tours: If snorkeling isn't your thing, you can still marvel at the reef's beauty through glass-bottom boat tours.

Sea Kayaking: Rent a sea kayak and paddle around the island's pristine coastline for a unique perspective.

Relaxation: Fitzroy Island is a haven for relaxation, so unwind on the sandy beaches or enjoy a leisurely picnic.

Cape Tribulation:
Where Rainforest Meets Reef

Venture north from Cairns, and you'll reach Cape Tribulation, where two UNESCO World Heritage sites, the Great Barrier Reef and the Daintree Rainforest, meet:

Daintree Discovery Centre: Start your exploration at the Daintree Discovery Centre, which offers a treetop walk and informative exhibits about the rainforest.

Cape Tribulation Beach: Stroll along the stunning Cape Tribulation Beach, where rainforest-clad mountains meet the sandy shores.

River Cruises: Take a river cruise on the Daintree River for the chance to spot crocodiles and other wildlife.

Guided Rainforest Tours: Join guided rainforest walks to learn about the unique flora and fauna of the Daintree.

Exploring the Outback: Undara Lava Tubes

For a unique outback adventure, head west from Cairns to the Undara Lava Tubes:

Undara Volcanic National Park: Explore the fascinating lava tubes formed by volcanic eruptions millions of years ago. Guided tours are available.

Wildlife Watching: Undara is a great place for birdwatching and spotting native wildlife in the Australian outback.

Bushwalks: Embark on bushwalks through the national park, where you can experience the rugged beauty of the outback landscape.

The Undiscovered Gem: Babinda Boulders

Just an hour's drive south of Cairns, the Babinda Boulders are a hidden gem known for their stunning natural beauty:

Swimming Holes: Cool off in the crystal-clear waters of the swimming holes formed by massive granite boulders.

Rainforest Walks: Explore the surrounding rainforest with walking trails that lead you to viewpoints and serene spots.

Cultural Significance: Learn about the indigenous Yidinji people and the cultural significance of this area.

These nearby destinations offer a diverse range of experiences, from relaxation and luxury to adventure and cultural immersion.

Whether you choose to visit Port Douglas, Palm Cove, Fitzroy Island, Cape Tribulation, Undara, or the Babinda Boulders, you're in for a memorable day trip from Cairns.

In the upcoming chapters, we'll provide practical tips to ensure a smooth and enjoyable visit to Cairns and its surroundings.

Chapter 9

PRACTICAL TIPS AND SAFETY

In this chapter, we'll cover essential practical tips and safety guidelines to ensure a smooth and enjoyable visit to Cairns. From staying safe to managing your finances, communication, local laws, and environmental responsibility, I've got you covered.

Staying Safe in Cairns: Health and Safety Guidelines

Cairns is a safe destination, but it's essential to follow some general safety guidelines:

Sun Protection: The Australian sun can be intense. Use sunscreen, wear a hat, and protect your eyes with sunglasses to avoid sunburn.

Marine Safety: When snorkeling or diving in the Great Barrier Reef, always listen to your guides, follow safety instructions, and be aware of your surroundings.

Wildlife Caution: While encounters with dangerous wildlife are rare, it's wise to be cautious. Don't approach or feed wildlife, especially crocodiles.

Swimming: Follow local advice and only swim in designated safe areas. Be mindful of stinger season (November to May) when jellyfish can be present. Consider wearing a stinger suit for protection.

Health Precautions: Check with your healthcare provider for recommended vaccinations and health precautions before your trip.

Money Matters: Currency Exchange and ATMs

Australia's currency is the Australian Dollar (AUD). Here's what you need to know about managing your finances in Cairns:

Currency Exchange: Currency exchange services are available at Cairns Airport, banks, and exchange offices in the city center. ATMs are another option for obtaining local cash.

ATMs: ATMs are widely available in Cairns, including at major banks, shopping centers, and tourist areas. Be aware of any foreign transaction fees your bank may charge.

Credit Cards: Major credit cards like Visa and MasterCard are widely accepted. However, it's a good idea to carry some cash for small purchases or places that may not accept cards.

Communication and Internet Access

Staying connected while in Cairns is easy:

Mobile Network: Australia has a reliable mobile network. If you have an unlocked phone, you can purchase a local SIM card for data and calls.

Wi-Fi: Most hotels, cafes, and restaurants in Cairns offer free Wi-Fi for customers. Additionally, you can find public Wi-Fi hotspots in some parks and public areas.

Emergency Services: In case of emergencies, dial 000 for police, fire, or medical assistance.

Local Laws and Etiquette

Understanding local laws and etiquette is essential for a respectful and enjoyable visit:

Alcohol Laws: Drinking in public places, except in licensed areas, is generally not allowed.

Smoking: Smoking is prohibited in many public places, including restaurants, bars, and indoor areas. Make sure to look for areas where smoking is permitted.

Respect for Indigenous Culture: When visiting indigenous sites or cultural centers, respect local customs and traditions. Always get consent before taking a picture.

Littering: Dispose of trash in designated bins. Cairns places a strong emphasis on environmental responsibility.

Tipping: Tipping is not as common in Australia as in some other countries. While it's appreciated, it's not mandatory. If you receive excellent service, a 10% tip is a common practice.

Environmental Responsibility: Protecting the Reef and Rainforest

Cairns is surrounded by fragile ecosystems, including the Great Barrier Reef and the Daintree Rainforest. Here's how you can help ensure their survival:

Eco-Friendly Tours: Choose tour operators who follow sustainable and eco-friendly practices when exploring the reef and rainforest.

Reduce Plastic Use: Minimize your plastic waste by using reusable water bottles and bags. Cairns has refill stations for water bottles.

Coral-Safe Sunscreen: When snorkeling or swimming in the reef, use coral-safe sunscreen to protect both yourself and the delicate ecosystem.

Respect Nature: When hiking or exploring, stay on designated paths and follow Leave No Trace principles to minimize your impact on the environment.

Wildlife Viewing: Keep a safe distance from wildlife and avoid feeding them, as it can disrupt their natural behaviors.

By adhering to these practical tips and safety guidelines, you'll have a safe and enjoyable experience in Cairns while also doing your part to protect its stunning natural surroundings.

In the upcoming chapter, I'll provide itineraries tailored to various types of travelers, so you can make the most of your Cairns adventure.

Get ready for more exploration!

Chapter 10

ITINERARIES FOR EVERY TRAVELER

Cairns offers something for every type of traveler, whether you're an adventure seeker, nature enthusiast, family vacationer, romantic at heart, or a solo explorer.

In this chapter, we'll help you tailor your Cairns adventure with itineraries designed to suit your travel style.

One-Week Adventure: A Quick Taste of Cairns

If you have one week to spare, you can experience the best of Cairns and its surroundings. Here's a sample itinerary:

Day 1: Arrival in Cairns

Arrive in Cairns and settle into your accommodation.

Explore the Cairns Esplanade and enjoy a leisurely evening stroll along the waterfront.

Day 2: Great Barrier Reef

Embark on a full-day snorkeling or diving tour to the Great Barrier Reef.

Explore vibrant coral gardens and swim with exotic marine life.

Day 3: Rainforest Discovery

Take a day trip to the Daintree Rainforest and Cape Tribulation.

Enjoy a guided rainforest walk and visit the stunning Mossman Gorge.

Day 4: Fitzroy Island

Catch a ferry to Fitzroy Island.

Spend the day snorkeling, hiking, or simply relaxing on the island's pristine beaches.

Day 5: Kuranda Village

Visit the quaint Kuranda Village via the Skyrail Rainforest Cableway.

Explore the markets and take a journey on the Kuranda Scenic Railway.

Day 6: Atherton Tablelands

Venture to the Atherton Tablelands.

Visit waterfalls like Millaa Millaa Falls and sample local cheese at dairy farms.

Day 7: Departure

Spend your last morning in Cairns at leisure.

Depart Cairns with unforgettable memories of your adventure.

Two-Week Explorer: Delving Deeper into Cairns and Beyond

With two weeks, you can immerse yourself even further into Cairns and its surroundings. Here's a more extensive itinerary:

Days 1-7: As per the One-Week Adventure Itinerary

Day 8-10: Port Douglas

Drive to Port Douglas and spend three days exploring the town and its attractions.

Visit the Great Barrier Reef again from this charming coastal town.

Day 11-13: Palm Cove

Continue your journey to Palm Cove for relaxation and beachfront luxury.

Take a day trip to nearby attractions or simply unwind by the sea.

Day 14-17: Cape Tribulation and Daintree

Drive north to Cape Tribulation and spend four days delving into the Daintree Rainforest.

Explore jungle trails, visit indigenous cultural centers, and enjoy boat cruises along the Daintree River.

Day 18-20: Fitzroy Island and Babinda Boulders

Return to Cairns briefly before heading to Fitzroy Island for relaxation.

Conclude your adventure with a visit to the Babinda Boulders, a hidden gem.

Family-Friendly Cairns: Activities for Kids

Cairns is a fantastic destination for families. Here's a family-friendly itinerary:

Days 1-3: Arrival and Cairns

Arrive in Cairns and settle into family-friendly accommodation.

Explore the Cairns Esplanade and the Muddy's Playground.

Day 4-5: Great Barrier Reef

Take a family-friendly reef tour with options for snorkeling and glass-bottom boat rides.

Day 6: Rainforest and Wildlife

Visit the Rainforestation Nature Park for an interactive wildlife experience.

Day 7-9: Fitzroy Island

Spend three days on Fitzroy Island, where kids can enjoy snorkeling, hiking, and beachcombing.

Day 10-12: Kuranda and Atherton Tablelands

Explore Kuranda Village, including the Australian Butterfly Sanctuary.

Head to the Atherton Tablelands for family-friendly outdoor activities.

Day 13-14: Departure

Spend your last day in Cairns at leisure.

Depart Cairns with happy memories of family adventures.

Romantic Getaway: Cairns for Couples

Cairns sets the scene for a romantic escape. Here's a romantic itinerary:

Days 1-3: Arrival and Cairns

Arrive in Cairns and check into a romantic waterfront hotel or resort.

Enjoy intimate dinners at Cairns' fine dining restaurants.

Day 4-6: Great Barrier Reef

Embark on a private or small-group reef tour.

Savor a romantic day of snorkeling, diving, or simply lounging on the reef.

Day 7-9: Port Douglas

Drive to Port Douglas for a romantic getaway.

Explore the town's art galleries, dine at beachfront restaurants, and relax on Four Mile Beach.

Day 10-12: Daintree Rainforest

Retreat to a rainforest lodge in the Daintree.

Explore the lush rainforest, take a river cruise, and stargaze in the wilderness.

Day 13-14: Departure

Spend your last day in Cairns at leisure.

Depart Cairns with cherished memories of your romantic journey.

Solo Traveler's Cairns: Embrace the Adventure

Traveling solo in Cairns is an adventure waiting to happen. Here's a solo traveler's itinerary:

Days 1-3: Arrival and Cairns

Arrive in Cairns and stay in a sociable hostel or boutique hotel.

Join group tours or meet fellow travelers at Cairns' backpacker bars.

Day 4-6: Great Barrier Reef

Join a group reef tour to meet fellow travelers and share the underwater experience.

Day 7-9: Cape Tribulation

Head north to Cape Tribulation for rainforest adventures and group activities.

Day 10-12: Port Douglas and Palm Cove

Spend a few days in Port Douglas and Palm Cove, where you can relax or join group tours to the reef or rainforest.

Day 13-14: Departure

Spend your last day in Cairns at leisure.

Depart Cairns with new friends and unforgettable solo adventures.

Whether you're traveling with family, a partner, or going solo, Cairns offers a tailored itinerary for every traveler.

In the next and final chapter, we'll conclude your journey with some parting thoughts and encourage you to continue exploring the world.

Get ready to wrap up your unforgettable Cairns adventure!

Chapter 11

RESOURCES AND ADDITIONAL INFORMATION

As you prepare for your Cairns adventure, having the right resources at your fingertips can make your journey smoother and more enjoyable.

In this chapter, we'll provide you with a valuable toolkit to enhance your Cairns travel experience.

Useful Websites and Apps for Cairns Travel

Tourism Tropical North Queensland: The official website for tourism in Cairns and the surrounding region. It's a goldmine of information on activities, accommodations, and local events.

Website: www.tropicalnorthqueensland.org.au

Cairns Airport: Stay updated on flight information, terminal facilities, and transport options to and from the airport.

Website: www.cairnsairport.com.au

TransLink: For information on public transportation services in and around Cairns, including bus and ferry schedules.

Website: translink.com.au

Cairns Post: Keep up with local news and events happening in Cairns and the Far North Queensland region.

Website: www.cairnspost.com.au

Cairns Local Weather: Stay informed about the latest weather conditions in Cairns and the surrounding areas.

App: Various weather apps are available for real-time updates.

Booking Tours and Activities

Viator: A popular platform for booking tours and activities in Cairns and worldwide.

Website: www.viator.com

TripAdvisor: Read reviews and book tours, excursions, and activities based on traveler feedback.

Website: www.tripadvisor.com

Cairns Tours and Attractions: A local booking platform offering a wide range of tours and activities in the Cairns region.

Website: www.cairnstoursandattractions.com.au

Airbnb Experiences: Discover unique, locally hosted activities and experiences in Cairns.

Website: www.airbnb.com/experiences

Local Tour Operators: Many local operators have their own websites for booking directly. Check for operators specializing in reef and rainforest tours, as well as other adventures.

Traveler's Checklist: What Not to Forget

Before embarking on your Cairns adventure, don't forget to:

Check Passport and Visa: Ensure your passport is valid for at least six months beyond your intended departure date. Check visa requirements for your nationality.

Travel Insurance: Purchase comprehensive travel insurance that covers medical emergencies, trip cancellations, and any activities you plan to do in Cairns.

Health Precautions: Consult your healthcare provider for recommended vaccinations and health precautions, and pack any necessary medications.

Pack Light and Smart: Cairns has a relaxed vibe, so pack light, comfortable clothing suitable for warm weather.

Don't forget swimwear, sunscreen, and insect repellent.

Adapters and Chargers: Bring power adapters and chargers for your devices. Australia uses Type I plugs with 230V electricity.

Travel Documents: Carry printed or digital copies of your flight itineraries, hotel reservations, and any tour bookings.

Local Currency: Have some Australian Dollars (AUD) in cash for small purchases or places that may not accept cards.

Emergency Contacts: Save the contact information for local authorities, your country's embassy or consulate, and your travel insurance provider.

Reader's Stories: Personal Cairns Adventures

Cairns has a way of creating unforgettable memories for travelers. Share your personal Cairns adventures, tips, and photos with fellow travelers on social media platforms, travel forums, or personal blogs.

Your stories can inspire others to explore this tropical paradise.

Contact Information for Local Authorities and Embassies

In case of emergencies or if you need assistance, here are some important contact numbers and locations:

Emergency Services: Dial 000 for police, fire, or medical assistance.

Cairns Visitor Information Centre:

Address: Cnr Aplin and The Esplanade, Cairns, QLD 4870

Phone: +61 7 4031 1751

Embassies and Consulates: If you're in need of consular assistance from your home country, contact your embassy or consulate in Australia.

Here are some embassy locations:

United States Embassy in Canberra:

https://au.usembassy.gov/

United Kingdom High Commission in Canberra: https://www.gov.uk/world/organisations/british-high-commission-canberra

Canadian High Commission in Canberra:

https://www.canadainternational.gc.ca/australia-australie/index.aspx?lang=eng

As you wrap up your Cairns adventure, remember that this incredible tropical paradise will always welcome you back.

Whether you're drawn to the Great Barrier Reef, the Daintree Rainforest, or the vibrant culture of Cairns, there's always more to explore.

Continue your travel journey with newfound experiences and memories, and let your adventures never cease.

Safe travels!

Conclusion

FAREWELL TO CAIRNS: A MEMORABLE EXPERIENCE

It's time to take stock of the amazing adventure you've experienced in this tropical paradise as we say goodbye to Cairns.

Your heart and spirit have been permanently changed by the vibrant combination of natural beauty, a thriving cultural community, and adventure opportunities in Cairns. You've seen the best that nature has to offer, from the splendors of the Great Barrier Reef to the eerie mysteries of the Daintree Rainforest.

You have created a tapestry of memories that you will treasure forever thanks to the cultural immersion, outdoor experiences, and culinary delights.

Sharing Your Cairns Adventure

We want you to tell other travelers about your Cairns adventure. Your ideas, images, and tales may motivate others to go out on their own journeys. Connecting with a worldwide community of tourists keen to discover Cairns may be done quite effectively through social media platforms, travel blogs, and discussion forums.

Others can benefit from your suggestions and personal tales to make the most of their time in this tropical paradise.

Keep Exploring:
Your Travel Journey Continues

Although your time in Cairns may be coming to an end, your travels are far from over. There are innumerable places to visit all around the world.

As you proceed, keep in mind the knowledge and experiences you have received in Cairns, such as the value of environmental conservation, the depth of cultural immersion, and the excitement of outdoor discovery.

As you travel to new places, keep these lessons in mind to inspire awe and respect for the rich diversity of our planet.

With its stunning natural surroundings and welcoming people, Cairns will always be a memorable holiday destination. But as one journey comes to an end, another calls.

So keep exploring, keep learning, and keep appreciating the beauty of our planet whether you're going to a humming city, a peaceful mountain retreat, or another far-flung locale.

The world is your oyster as you continue your travels.

Printed in Great Britain
by Amazon